SPYING, SURVEILLANCE, AND
PRIVACY IN THE 21st CENTURY

Mass Government Surveillance
Spying on Citizens

Andrew Coddington

Cavendish Square

New York

Published in 2018 by Cavendish Square Publishing, LLC
243 5th Avenue, Suite 136, New York, NY 10016

Copyright © 2018 by Cavendish Square Publishing, LLC

First Edition

Library of Congress Cataloging-in-Publication Data

Names: Coddington, Andrew.
Title: Mass government surveillance / Andrew Coddington.
Description: New York : Cavendish Square Publishing, 2018. | Series:
Spying, surveillance, and privacy in the 21st-century | Includes index.
Identifiers: ISBN 9781502626721 (library bound) | ISBN 9781502626677 (ebook)
Subjects: LCSH: Espionage--United States--Juvenile literature. | Intelligence service--United States--Juvenile literature. | United States.--National Security Agency--Juvenile literature.
Classification: LCC JK468.I6 K55 2018 | DDC 363.325'1630973--dc23

Editorial Director: David McNamara
Editor: Fletcher Doyle
Copy Editor: Nathan Heidelberger
Associate Art Director: Amy Greenan
Designer: Stephanie Flecha
Production Coordinator: Karol Szymczuk
Photo Research: J8 Media

Printed in the United States of America

Contents

Governments looking to protect their citizens have increased mass surveillance, but it poses the question: Are these programs worth it?

CHAPTER 1

Liberty and Security in America

One of the primary responsibilities of any government is to protect its citizens. Many political philosophers—particularly those active during the Enlightenment, a period during the seventeenth and eighteenth centuries in Europe that saw great development in the fields of moral and political philosophy—argue that the duty to protect is the most fundamental expectation a citizen has for the government. Enlightenment thinkers such as Jean-Jacques Rousseau and John Locke insisted on the idea of a "social contract" between each citizen and his or her government. Rather than an actual paper document signed by tens of thousands or millions of individuals, this "contract" is an implicit understanding that a citizen will curb some of his or her natural liberties, such as the ability to assault someone and steal his or her property, in order to assimilate into a society where other individuals agree to do the same. The society, meanwhile, will agree to protect those who uphold their end of the contract while also prosecuting those who do not.

The social contract is basically an exchange of liberty for personal security, but it does not specify how much liberty an individual is required to sacrifice, nor how much security a government can reasonably guarantee. This problem proves tricky because there are many governments today that have guaranteed their citizens a certain degree of the right to privacy but that are starting to face increased pressure to protect their citizens from crime, warfare, and **terrorism**.

How far can a government go toward protecting its citizens while also respecting their freedom? How much can invading someone's privacy really help in protecting a nation? These questions have only gotten more puzzling as technology has improved over the last few decades. The right to privacy is no longer thought to be limited to people's homes and belongings. Instead, some argue it now expands to include their digital lives, including their phone, text, and email conversations, as well as documents stored on computers or in the cloud. Meanwhile, the advancement of technology also means that it is that much easier for governments to conduct mass **surveillance** operations—and also for criminals and terrorists to conceal their plans. This cat-and-mouse game between well-meaning government agencies and wrongdoers often puts ordinary citizens in the cross fire.

Surveillance in Prerevolutionary America

The debate over the reasonable expectation of privacy in America has roots in the American Revolution and even the settlement of the New World. When English colonists first arrived in America, they carried with them the sorts of ideas that helped shape the political evolution of Great Britain, which had at that point only recently undergone a

Americans increasingly store personal information and conduct their personal lives over the internet, thanks to connected devices such as smartphones.

significant democratization in which the monarchy agreed to share some of its power with the common people. In addition, many colonists, such as the Puritans arriving in New England and Catholic immigrants in Maryland, were traveling to America in order to escape religious persecution at the hands of the Anglican elite in England. These groups hoped that America might allow them freedom to practice their religion without government intervention or harassment.

When the relationship between Great Britain and its North American colonies started to sour during the eighteenth century, a new facet of American liberty took root. The British had recently fought and won the French and Indian War, in which the British defeated their rivals in North America, the French and their Native American allies. However, this victory came at a great price. In order the defray the cost of the war, as well as to improve security in the North American colonies, Parliament passed two quartering acts. The Quartering Act of 1765 required that the American colonists provide room and board to any British troops who needed it in the event that the soldiers stationed in the colonies outnumbered the space available in military barracks. Although the first Quartering Act stopped short of requiring regular colonists to house soldiers in their own homes, the bill specified that inns, taverns, and the private residences of alcohol merchants, as well as outbuildings on private property, such as barns, could be forced into service as makeshift housing for soldiers with local governments footing the soldiers' bills for food, drink, and rent.

Parliament saw the first Quartering Act as a practical way of supporting the colonies' first standing army to deter the French. At the same time, Parliament hoped the act would reduce the strain on Britain's coffers by displacing some of the cost to the colonial governments, which the British people widely felt did not play a large enough role (or pay enough money) in the defense of their own lands.

To the colonists, however, the prospect of hosting what were essentially foreign troops in their backyard and financing their quartering through taxes was understandably undesirable. In New York, where the largest number of British troops were stationed, resentment over the Quartering Act was particularly high. In January 1766, the New York Assembly voted against funding the full amount requested by Parliament to support its troops, sparking months of bickering between colonial and royal officials. In the fall, the assembly voted against funding the troops at all, which prompted the British to suspend New York's colonial government entirely. Although tensions were high, the matter in New York eventually dissipated when New York voted to supply funds for the troops.

The strained relationship between Great Britain and the North American colonies worsened as Parliament continued to pass a series of acts levying taxes against the colonists in order to defray the debts it had accumulated during the French and Indian War. One such law was the Tea Act, which enforced a duty on tea that had been exported to the colonies. The Tea Act was so reviled that it sparked a group of American patriots in Boston, Massachusetts, to board three British merchant ships docked in Boston Harbor and destroy 340 chests of tea valued at £9,659 (over $1.7 million in today's money) by throwing them into the water.

The Boston Tea Party, as it came to be known, infuriated the British, who took severe steps toward quelling the

British encroachment on the homes of Americans was among the issues that started the American Revolution.

bubbling revolution. Parliament passed a series of laws that became known in the colonies as the Intolerable Acts. Among those was the second Quartering Act, passed in 1774, which allowed British governors to station troops directly in private residences, especially in Massachusetts. The second Quartering Act was equal parts practical and punitive. On the one hand, it essentially instituted martial law in Boston, installing a red-coated overseer in practically every home. The presence of armed troops in colonial America's most volatile city was expected to reduce revolutionary sentiment by preventing patriots from organizing and plotting against the royal government there. On the other hand, at the same time the Quartering Act was eliminating American privacy, it did not include a provision in which homeowners would be reimbursed, meaning that every American hosting a British soldier had to pay for his "guest's" expenses out of pocket.

The pushback against the Quartering Acts demonstrated the American colonies' reluctance to allow government into their homes, a sentiment which would crop up again and again throughout the history of the United States.

Defining Privacy in the New Nation

Aggressive parliamentary laws like the Quartering Acts eventually pushed the American colonies into war with Great Britain, which effectively ended in October 1781 when the British general Charles Cornwallis surrendered to George Washington at the Battle of Yorktown in Virginia. The Treaty of Paris formally recognized America's independence two years later. In the aftermath of a complete separation from its mother country, the United States was met with an unprecedented opportunity to craft a national government from the ground up. With the memory of British rule and the goals of the Revolution fresh in mind, the new American states began work on devising a system that would champion individual liberty and unite the separate states under one limited government.

The Continental Congress tried to create this vision at first by ratifying the Articles of Confederation, the first

constitution of the United States, on November 15, 1777, but the articles' imperfect balance of liberty and authority was immediately apparent. Under the Articles of Confederation, each of the thirteen states elected representatives to a unicameral legislature, which was the only government at the national level. Because this federal legislature did not also have an executive branch that would carry out the laws it passed, the individual states were essentially sovereign nations operating outside the jurisdiction of Congress. As a case in point, it took until March 1, 1781—nearly four years after the articles were passed—for the last state to ratify them.

The independence of each state led to significant imbalances in terms of laws and taxes between neighboring states, which in turn sparked dissent among Americans. Several small-scale insurrections, such as Shays's Rebellion in Massachusetts, cropped up. Just years after winning independence, it seemed America was slipping into a state of anarchy.

Many Americans began recognizing the need for a stronger centralized government with the power necessary to ensure relative equality among the states and enforce order and security. Those that supported a new government came to be called Federalists and included such thinkers as John Adams and Alexander Hamilton. They argued that if America were to survive as a nation and succeed in the world, then a new constitution in which the central government had authority over the constituent states would have to be written. This argument won out at the Constitutional Convention in 1787, and the new Constitution took effect on March 4, 1789, replacing the Articles of Confederation. Under this new government, the states elected representatives to a bicameral legislature called Congress, divided into the lower

George Washington leads troops to stop the Whiskey Rebellion. *The Whiskey Rebellion* was painted circa 1795.

House of Representatives and the higher Senate. Laws passed by Congress would be carried out by the executive branch, headed by the president, who oversaw the administrative bureaucracy. As a guarantee that neither Congress nor the president would overstep their bounds, a judiciary branch known as the Supreme Court was formed with the power to review the actions of the other branches.

Checking Federal Power

While the Articles of Confederation were widely believed to have been too lax, many Americans, such as Thomas Jefferson, who wrote the Declaration of Independence (along with John Adams), feared that the pendulum of power at the Constitutional Convention might swing too far over into authoritarianism. Jefferson in particular feared that the values of the American Revolution might be lost entirely, and that Americans, for want of security, might end up ratifying a government modeled after the monarchy that they had just fought so desperately to escape. Those who agreed with Jefferson assembled under America's second political party, named the Democratic-Republicans.

In 1791, a staunch Democratic-Republican and protégé of Thomas Jefferson named James Madison proposed a solution to the problem of federal authority. At the same time that the Constitution consolidated power in the national government, Congress would also ratify a **Bill of Rights** that enumerated those liberties that would be due to individuals and states. The Bill of Rights takes the form of the first ten **amendments** to the Constitution.

The Right to Privacy

Contrary to popular belief, the United States does not offer any guarantees of privacy to its citizens under the Constitution, but many legal scholars believe that there is an *implied* right to privacy contained within several of the amendments in the Bill of Rights. Several of these seem to be direct responses to the violations of privacy perpetrated by the British under the Quartering Acts. The Third Amendment, for example, explicitly prohibits the quartering of soldiers in private residences without the permission of the homeowner during peacetime, and in war only "in a manner to be prescribed by law."

Many scholars look to the Fourth Amendment as further indication of a reasonable expectation of privacy. It reads:

> The right of the people to be secure in their persons, houses, papers, and effects, against unreasonable searches and seizures, shall not be violated, and no warrants shall issue, but upon probable cause, supported by oath or affirmation, and particularly describing the place to be searched, and the persons or things to be seized.

The amendment states that law enforcement officials must obtain search warrants during their investigation of a crime and that these warrants may only be granted when there is "probable cause." Probable cause is a degree of certainty that suggests a person is guilty of or otherwise connected to a crime. All of this is to say that a police officer or other law enforcement officials cannot randomly or specifically stop an individual or search their home and belongings unless there is preexisting evidence that that person has committed a crime.

The Fifth Amendment protects the rights of those accused of crimes. In particular, this amendment protects a person from serving as a "witness against himself," meaning that a person cannot be forced to self-incriminate or provide evidence that is not in his or her favor. Scholars believe that this amendment favors privacy because it can extend to protect personal information.

Lastly, the Ninth Amendment is also thought by many to protect privacy, because it states, "The enumeration in the Constitution, of certain rights, shall not be construed to deny or disparage others retained by the people." The vagueness of this amendment seems to defy interpretation. On the one hand, it may very likely have been included to serve as a doorway for future amendments protecting individual and state liberties. However, Supreme Court Justice Arthur Goldberg, writing his opinion for the case *Griswold v. Connecticut* (1965), argued that the Ninth Amendment includes those rights that, though unwritten, are supported by the values and practices of American society.

The most frequently quoted statement by a Supreme Court justice on the subject of privacy comes in Justice Louis Brandeis's dissent in *Olmstead v. United States* (1928):

> The makers of our Constitution undertook to secure conditions favorable to the pursuit of happiness. They recognized the significance of man's spiritual nature, of his feelings, and of his intellect. They knew that only a part of the pain, pleasure and satisfactions of life are to be found in material things. They sought to protect Americans in their beliefs, their thoughts, their emotions and their sensations. They conferred, as against the Government, the right to be let alone— the most comprehensive of rights, and the right most valued by civilized men. To protect that right, every unjustifiable intrusion by the Government upon the privacy of the individual, whatever the means employed, must be deemed a violation of the Fourth Amendment.

Surveillance in the Civil War

The values and ideals of privacy expressed in the Bill of Rights were tested by the realities of running a nation practically as soon as they were written. Just as the British had found in the lead-up to the American Revolution, the practical benefits of violating liberty in the interest of protecting the nation proved tempting to the new United States government.

Ironically, one of the earliest threats to the American concept of privacy was enacted by one of history's greatest proponents of civil rights: President Abraham Lincoln. At the time of Lincoln's candidacy, the United States was deeply divided on the issue of slavery. States in the North began to demand the practice be abolished, while the Southern states, whose plantation economy at the time depended on the labor of slaves, complained that their interests were not being fairly represented at the national level. The issue came to a head within weeks of Lincoln's election, as South Carolina became the first state to secede from the Union on December 20, 1860, and several other slaveholding states followed South Carolina's lead in the following months. Less than a century after America had declared independence from Great Britain, it seemed the country was again headed for a rebellion that would tear the country apart. The need to compel the rebel states to rejoin the Union sparked the Civil War.

There is no question that the situation faced by President Lincoln was unprecedented. Although George Washington had been faced with rebellion during his time as president, the "Whiskey Rebellion," so-called because it arose out of protest to the new federal government's tax on liquor, was isolated to the western part of Pennsylvania and limited to a few hundred men. Lincoln's crisis included eleven rebel states that joined an organized Confederacy with a population totaling nearly ten million. In addition, the secession of Virginia on April 17, 1861, proved especially problematic. Virginia is situated directly to the south of the Potomac River, adjacent to Washington, DC, and Maryland, which at the time remained with the Union but nevertheless harbored Confederate sympathizers. Should Maryland fall to the rebels, the capital of the Union would be surrounded.

On May 25, 1861, Lincoln's fears were in part realized. A Maryland militia leader named John Merryman destroyed railroad lines leading through Baltimore County, effectively halting the transport of Union troops to the South and undermining the Union's war effort. Federal officers arrested Merryman on charges of treason. Later accusations against Merryman included threatening Union soldiers camped near his estate, burning a bridge used by Union troops, destroying telegraph lines to sever Union communications, and advocating secessionist principles to soldiers under his command. Merryman was held at Fort McHenry without trial.

In order to neutralize Merryman and keep Maryland on the side of the Union, President Lincoln wrote to General Winfield Scott, authorizing him to suspend the **writ of habeas corpus**. Habeas corpus, which in Latin translates to "you shall have the body," is a legal protection that allows a person detained for a crime to have their charges reviewed by a court. This suspension, Lincoln wrote, would apply to "all persons arrested, or who are now, or hereafter during the rebellion shall be, imprisoned in any fort, camp, arsenal, military prison, or other place of confinement by any military authority." As justification for the suspension of this civil right, Lincoln said that doing so was a "necessary measure for suppressing … all rebels and insurgents, their aiders and abettors, within the United States, and all persons … guilty of any disloyal practice."

When Merryman's attorney requested a writ of habeas corpus, Chief Justice Roger Taney complied, commanding Merryman's captors to present him before the Supreme Court. However, the federal officers refused, citing Lincoln's order to General Scott as justification. Taney wrote an opinion arguing that Lincoln had no such authority. The right to habeas corpus is constitutionally guaranteed, but the Constitution also allows for it to be suspended "when in cases of rebellion and invasion the public safety may require it" under Article I, Section 9 (also called the "suspension clause"). However, constitutionally speaking, the suspension clause is included in the part of the Constitution enumerating legislative, not executive, powers. Furthermore, because the ability to suspend habeas corpus is not expressly granted to the president, it automatically belongs to Congress.

Lincoln ignored Taney's argument, and neither the Supreme Court nor any lower federal courts were ever involved in the issue again.

The effects of Lincoln's precedent have been profound. Because the issue was never concluded, the power to suspend habeas corpus resides with both Congress and the president. Although the Supreme Court may still check the actions of the president (though they have not since Lincoln), the president can justify the suspension of habeas corpus only if it proves to be necessary to the security of the United States. In other words, a citizen may be lawfully detained and held without trial if doing so is vital to national security. This precedent has been widely cited to justify actions of the president during times of national emergency, suggesting that, perhaps contrary to the Bill of Rights, national security trumps individual liberties.

President Richard Nixon was forced to resign for his role in the illegal surveillance of political rivals.

Privacy in the Modern Era:
The Watergate Scandal

In the early morning of June 17, 1972, police officers arrested five burglars who had broken into the offices of the Democratic National Committee (DNC) at the Watergate complex in Washington, DC. Among those taken into custody was a man named James W. McCord Jr., who

The Stakes of Surveillance

America has entered a new era in the privacy/surveillance debate. The proliferation of internet-connected technology has fundamentally changed the way people live. In 2015, the Pew Research Group found that 68 percent of Americans own a smartphone, including 83 percent of people between the ages of thirty and forty-nine, and 86 percent of people aged eighteen to twenty-nine. These devices are often filled with sensitive personal information, from bank and credit card accounts to social media interactions and internet search **data**.

Terrorists now operate without borders. From a law enforcement perspective, practically anyone can be **radicalized** and orchestrate another terrorist attack on the scale of 9/11.

This sea change has happened only recently, and its implications are only just starting to be understood and debated. Technology is a convenience that few of us would care to give up—46 percent of respondents to a Gallup survey agreed that they could not imagine their lives without their smartphones. On the one hand, there is an inborn expectation among Americans that they have a right to privacy and that their government will not rifle through their personal information. On the other hand, there is an expectation on government to keep us safe, which in the digital age seems to require a level of official snooping in our private lives.

We need to question how much access law enforcement officials should have, how effective surveillance programs are, how safe can we reasonably expect the government to keep us, and who we can trust. These are questions all of us are intimately involved in.

served as the security chief for a committee tasked with reelecting President Richard Nixon, who was a Republican. The break-in was initially reported in the *Washington Post* by two little-known journalists, Carl Bernstein and Bob Woodward. Shortly after the initial report, Woodward and Bernstein, along with Federal Bureau of Investigation (FBI) investigators, discovered the identities of two more men associated with the break-in: E. Howard Hunt Jr., a former Central Intelligence Agency (CIA) officer who was recently appointed to Nixon's staff, and G. Gordon Liddy, a former FBI agent who was working for Nixon's reelection committee. Given the number of connections to the White House, the press began questioning whether or not Nixon's reelection committee, the administration, or even Nixon himself was involved.

The White House denied any connection, and at first, press coverage doubted that the administration was connected. However, during this time, the conspirators began a process of destroying evidence, including tools used during the break-in, such as lock picks, radio scanners, and electronic devices known as "**bugs**" capable of secretly recording conversations, as well as transcripts of illegal **wiretaps** of DNC telephones. The White House also began drafting plans to secretly transport Hunt out of the country.

Suspicion that Nixon was involved in the surveillance was confirmed when leaked phone conversations revealed that Nixon had ordered the FBI to draw down its investigation. The discovery proved that Nixon himself was directly involved in the cover-up of a conspiracy to spy on the administration's political rivals at the DNC.

Woodward and Bernstein broke the news of what became known as the Watergate scandal thanks in part to an anonymous source identified only as "Deep Throat." (Thirty years after Watergate, "Deep Throat" was shown to be W. Mark Felt, who was then deputy director at the FBI.) Woodward and Bernstein confirmed that Watergate was just the tip of the iceberg, however, writing in an October 10 article:

> The Watergate bugging incident stemmed from a massive campaign of political spying and sabotage conducted on behalf of President Nixon's re-election and directed by officials of the White House.

The fallout of the Watergate scandal was as unprecedented as its cause: Nixon's complicity in a systematic domestic surveillance program designed to undermine political rivals eventually caused his popularity to plummet. Calls for his impeachment grew louder as the investigation revealed the scope of his involvement. Nixon announced his resignation on August 8, 1974, and he left office the next day.

The effects of Watergate are being felt in America even today. The revelations about the covert domestic surveillance program organized at the highest levels of government combined with the innate American mistrust of authority is likely part of the reason why Americans are so cynical about their government.

Surveillance in the Twenty-First Century: The USA PATRIOT Act

The defining event of the early part of the twenty-first century was the terrorist attack on the United States on September 11, 2001, and the declaration of the War on Terror by the United

Edward Snowden and the NSA Leak

On June 6, 2013, the United Kingdom–based newspaper the *Guardian* reported that the National Security Agency (NSA) was indiscriminately collecting the phone records of customers of the wireless carrier Verizon. A then-unknown **whistleblower** had leaked to the newspaper a classified court order mandating that the company deliver all of its information to the NSA on an "ongoing, daily basis." The following day, the *Guardian*, working off another leak, reported that a top-secret, undisclosed NSA program named PRISM had allowed the agency direct access to the servers of such tech giants as Microsoft, Apple, Google, Yahoo, Facebook, and others. Those companies denied cooperating with the government, alleging that the PRISM program had gained access without their knowledge. The leak took the form of a PowerPoint presentation that seemed to have been used to train intelligence officers on collecting personal and activity information about those companies' customers, including search history, email content, file transfers, live chat transcripts, and more.

On June 9, 2013, a former CIA analyst and NSA contractor named Edward Snowden, then hiding from authorities in a hotel room in Hong Kong, revealed himself to be the source of the leaks in an interview with the *Guardian*. Snowden had trained as a Special Forces recruit, worked with the NSA, and worked in IT security at the CIA. Snowden told the *Guardian* that in 2007, while with the CIA in Geneva, he became "disillusioned … about how my government functions and what its impact is in the world.

I realized that I was part of something that was doing far more harm than good." Snowden left the CIA in 2009 to work as a contractor for the private consulting firm Booz Allen Hamilton, which had won millions of dollars worth of top-secret contracts with the NSA. Snowden later admitted that he took the job with Booz Allen Hamilton because he wanted to collect evidence of government surveillance, and the company had access to classified information.

Before details of Snowden's identity became public, the United States government had charged the whistleblower with theft of government property, unauthorized communication of national defense information, and willful communication of classified communications intelligence, each of which is punishable by up to ten years in prison. When the government asked Chinese authorities to **extradite** the whistleblower later that month, Snowden left to seek **asylum** initially in Ecuador before settling in Moscow, Russia. In January 2017, Russia said he could stay for "a couple more years."

In addition to evidence of mass domestic surveillance at the hands of the US government, Snowden also leaked documents that showed the United States was hacking China, as well as European citizens and European Union officials, such as German chancellor Angela Merkel, according to the German newspaper *Der Spiegel*. Information gleaned from Snowden's leaks also pointed to the United Kingdom's NSA equivalent, the Government Communications Headquarters, performing wiretaps to intercept internet data.

The September 11 terrorist attacks on New York and Washington, DC, sparked the War on Terror.

States. That morning, members of the extremist group **al-Qaeda hijacked** four commercial airplanes and crashed two into the World Trade Center complex in Manhattan, New York, and one into the Pentagon in Arlington, Virginia. The fourth, United Airlines Flight 93, seemed to be on course for Washington, DC, probably intended for the White House or the Capitol. However, passengers attempted to wrestle control from the terrorists, who crashed the plane in an abandoned field in Pennsylvania. All died, but the plane didn't do any further damage. Nearly three thousand people died during the course of the 9/11 attacks, and today, many people, most of whom were first responders, suffer chronic illness as a result of airborne debris left by the crashes.

Congress declaring War on Terror

The attacks shocked not only the United States but also the world at large. In response, America, under the leadership of President George W. Bush, declared a worldwide "war on terror" aimed at wiping out al-Qaeda and other groups like it. Speaking to a joint session of Congress on September 20, 2001, President Bush declared, "Every nation in every region now has a decision to make. Either you are with us, or you are with the terrorists."

Bush's policy enjoyed wide support among Americans in the aftermath of 9/11. However, a few people, including human rights and civil liberties advocates, questioned the sorts of measures governments around the world would enact in order to carry out the mission. Many feared that America would return to the police state of the 1960s and 1970s, when government agencies spied on and harassed known critics of the Vietnam War.

President George W. Bush (*seated*) signs the USA PATRIOT Act into law.

Responding to the challenges of fighting an enemy without borders that operated in secret using the latest cyber technologies, Congress sought to empower government agencies involved in prosecuting the War on Terror by passing the **USA PATRIOT Act** in October 2001. The name of the act is an acronym that stands for "Uniting and Strengthening America by Providing Appropriate Tools Required to Intercept and Obstruct Terrorism." Among the provisions in the PATRIOT Act was a drawdown of restrictions placed on government agencies such as the Central Intelligence Agency, the Federal Bureau of Investigation, and the National Security Agency. This drawdown dictated the amount and sort of data that could be legally collected by those agencies. Under the new law, the government could utilize essentially any surveillance method for any length of time while investigating an individual suspected to be connected to a terrorist organization.

The National Security Agency has become the focus of the mass government surveillance debate.

CHAPTER 2

The Pros: No Harm Done

The choice between mass government surveillance or personal privacy represents a zero-sum game. When individuals enjoy greater privacy, there is less information government agencies can collect, which hamstrings those agencies' ability to investigate and prevent serious crimes and acts of terror. Because America cannot have both privacy and surveillance—because we cannot have our cake and eat it too—the argument basically boils down to a value judgment. What is more important, privacy or security?

To those in favor of mass government surveillance programs, the answer to that question leans heavily toward security. The modern era is fraught with danger, they argue; criminals, terrorist groups, and even rival foreign powers threaten to unravel the fabric of American society on a daily basis. Such enemies that seek to harm the United States plot day and night, seemingly without rest. In the words of former House Majority Leader Eric Cantor, a Republican from Virginia, on *CBS This Morning*, on June 10, 2013, "Right now, we know that there are active threats against the

United States. We have terrorist threats that continue. There are possible security incidences that continue. And that's just the world that we live in."

Increased pressure to prevent crimes and other acts of terrorism before they even occur presents such agencies with a public mandate to remain hypervigilant. Many belonging to the pro-surveillance camp argue that if gathering reliable intelligence helps law enforcement officers keep people safe, then it should follow that allowing government agencies to gather more intelligence should keep people more safe. America's enemies use every advantage at their disposal, including the internet, cell phones, and other modern technologies and innovations that help them to coordinate their plans and shroud them in secrecy. Because criminals and terrorists have evolved for the internet age, government agencies tasked with protecting law-abiding citizens from them must evolve as well. It is no longer sufficient to rely on conventional police work or outmoded technologies such as stationary surveillance cameras to catch criminals because many of the greatest threats to society are hatched in the darkest corners of digital space.

The New Battlefield

Modern mass surveillance programs, such as the NSA's PRISM program, were a product of the terrorist attacks on September 11 and the subsequent declaration of the War on Terror. From the beginning, the government understood that battling **jihadists** in the twenty-first century was to be an unconventional fight. Past wars were typically fought against a clearly defined enemy, such as the Nazis in World War II. For most wars throughout history, combatants tended

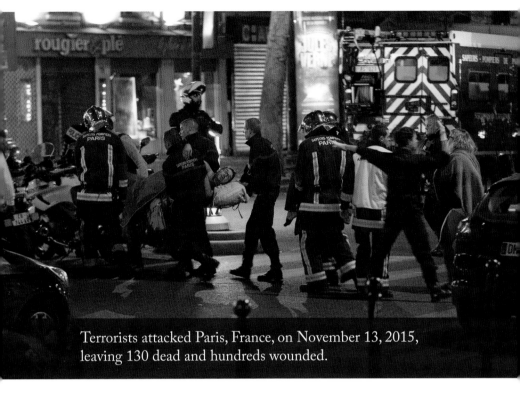

Terrorists attacked Paris, France, on November 13, 2015, leaving 130 dead and hundreds wounded.

to come from a single geographical location and typically identified themselves as belonging to one side or another through uniforms or other clear identifiers. The War on Terror, meanwhile, targets radical jihadist organizations, such as al-Qaeda, that are typically small collections of radicalized individuals operating out of remote parts of the world. Such groups are not generally bound by national identity or geographic location but rather belong to networks that span across the world, thanks in large part to the internet.

Because of their small numbers, terrorist organizations generally prefer premeditated strikes utilizing improvised weapons, such as pipe and car bombs, at locations with high potential for casualties, such as embassies and markets. If extremist groups do field soldiers, they are rarely if ever identifiable by uniforms, instead blending into the populace until they strike without warning.

The quickness of terrorist attacks allows for a very small window of opportunity to stop them once they have already started. This puts an increased pressure on militaries to stop such attacks well before they have the chance to begin. This requires the collection and analysis of large amounts of intelligence, which means more sophisticated and invasive surveillance networks.

A Changing Intelligence Landscape

The explosive improvement and integration of technology in society has given many people cause for concern. The ubiquity of internet-connected devices means that much of our most intimate personal information has been stored on the cloud: physical mail has been replaced by email, face-to-face conversations with text messages, and paper documents with digital ones. Each of these new technologies leaves a trail of cyber breadcrumbs, little bits and bytes that can be collected to form a convincing narrative about who you are, where you go, what you do, and potentially even what you want and how you think.

The changes in the way Americans conduct their lives has forced governments to change the way they conduct their investigations.

The Internet and the War on Terror

The War on Terror has been the first one fought at least in part in cyberspace. The problem of terrorist websites has only gotten worse in recent years. It's easy to see why: the same things that makes the internet so useful for ordinary people also makes it a valuable tool for terrorists. Online banking and fund transfer sites are convenient ways for civilians to organize and conduct their finances—and for extremist organizations to raise money. Message boards and social media platforms help civilians stay in touch with one another—and make it easy for terrorists to communicate with one another. Websites and blogs help regular people stay up to date with the latest news and trends—and allow terrorists to broadcast propaganda and recruit new members.

The internet is not only a natural convenience for terrorists; it also helps to conceal their work from the eyes of law enforcement. In the words of John Arquilla, professor of defense analysis at the Naval Postgraduate School in Monterey, California, "The greatest advantage of [the internet] is stealth … [Terrorists] swim in an ocean of bits and bytes." For one thing, communications sent over the internet can be exchanged and **encrypted** much more easily than in person. Throughout the history of warfare, rival forces have tried to veil their messages using complex codes known as ciphers so that the message appears to be a block of unreadable nonsense. Only those with a key can successfully translate the cipher and read it. Encryption helps conceal information in case correspondence falls into the hands of the enemy. With the internet, encryption has become second nature, with everyone from casual email users to top secret government agencies benefitting from encryption. In the case of terrorist communications, many groups use what is known as steganography, in which messages relayed in text are hidden within graphic files. Terrorists also use a technique known as "dead dropping," which doesn't even require encryption. Instead, terrorists may log into a shared email account in which they draft messages but do not send them. The messages are then saved in the password-protected account, available for any person with access to see, without the messages actually having to be transmitted. This eliminates the risk of interception.

More important to a radical extremist group than the internet's secrecy, however, is its ability to reach a wide audience. According to the Council on Foreign Relations, propaganda is the greatest cyber tool in the modern terrorist's arsenal. The internet allows even relatively small terrorist groups to post video recordings of statements by leaders, attacks, and executions of "enemy combatants," including especially the decapitations of hostages. Such videos can then be seen around the world. In addition to spreading fear and disrupting the day-to-day life of people from Baghdad to Brooklyn, these propaganda videos also help bolster resolve within the group and attract newcomers.

Fast Fact

According to a Department of Homeland Security white paper prepared in 2009, there were twelve terrorist websites active in 1998 but 6,940 active by January 2009. The book *Terrorism in Cyberspace: The Next Generation* by Gabriel Weimann reports that that number had grown to 9,800 by 2015. Weimann is a professor of communication at the University of Haifa, Israel.

Homegrown Extremism

It isn't called the "World Wide Web" for nothing. The internet connects people across the globe, which is both a positive and a negative, depending on how you look at it. In the case of the fight against terrorism, the interconnectedness that the internet offers is certainly a liability, as terrorist propaganda can potentially reach clear across the globe, including the United States itself.

Radical jihadist groups have seized on the opportunity to reach the masses. Among these is the Islamic State, also known as **ISIS** (Islamic State of Iraq and Syria) or occasionally ISIL (Islamic State of Iraq and the Levant), a group that grew out of an al-Qaeda cell in Iraq, eventually becoming a distinct organization. Tensions between al-Qaeda and what would become ISIS started to rise when al-Qaeda's leader, Ayman al-Zawahiri, admonished the leader of the Iraqi group, Abu Bakr al-Baghdadi, for unilaterally deciding to expand his group into Syria and take over the local al-Qaeda organization there. Zawahiri eventually disowned ISIS because the group's fundamentalist principles and brutal methods were considered too extreme even for al-Qaeda.

No other terrorist organization seems to capitalize on the marketing potential of the internet like ISIS has. The organization frequently publicizes videos depicting dozens of masked fighters in well-organized training demonstrations, battlefield footage of ISIS troops capturing towns, and executions of Western and pro-Western hostages. Perhaps the most dangerous innovation that ISIS has introduced into the War on Terror is the pioneering of so-called **lone wolf** attacks. Attacks of this nature are carried out by individuals who, though inspired by jihadist ideology and terrorist activity,

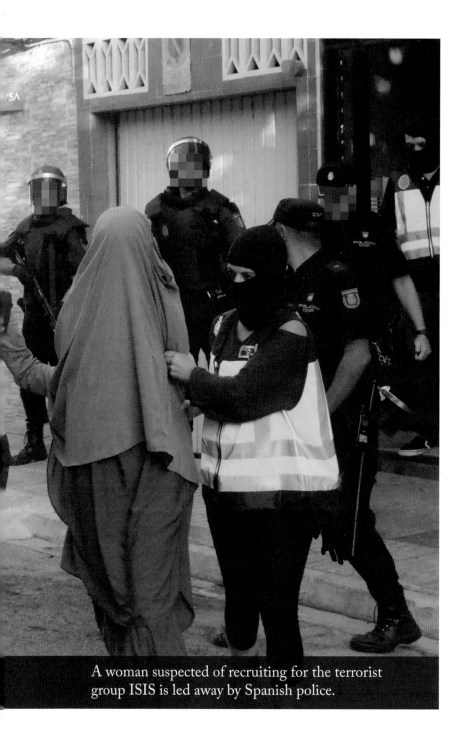

A woman suspected of recruiting for the terrorist group ISIS is led away by Spanish police.

do not have any sort of formal affiliation with any one group. Because there is no paper or digital trail linking known jihadist organizations with these individuals, it is difficult for law enforcement agencies to identify them. Practically anyone from any corner of the globe could be a radicalized lone wolf planning to strike.

In September 2014, ISIS released an audio recording in which a spokesman called for an escalation in precisely this activity:

> Hinder those who want to harm your brothers. The best thing you can do is to strive to do your best and kill any disbeliever, whether he be French, American, or from any of their allies … Rig the roads with explosives for them. Attack their bases. Raid their homes. Cut off their heads. Do not let them feel secure. Hunt them wherever they may be. Turn their worldly life into fear and fire. Remove their families from their homes and thereafter blow up their homes.

In addition to suggesting how an individual might advance ISIS's cause as his own, the recording specifically summons "faithful" Muslims living in the West to take the fight to the streets. In particular, the spokesman calls to action those Muslims living in the United States, which ISIS considers to be the greatest threat to Islam, as well as its allies in France and Australia.

The problem of homegrown jihadist terror within Western democracies has been the subject of many of the biggest headlines in recent history, from the shooting in San Bernardino, California, in December 2015 to the June

2016 massacre at Pulse nightclub in Orlando, Florida. Both attacks were carried out, at least in part, by American-born terrorists who had been inspired to action by jihadist propaganda similar to that published by ISIS. (The exception is the San Bernardino case, in which American-born Syed Rizwan Farook conspired with his wife, Tashfeen Malik, who had been born in Pakistan.)

Catching Boston Bombers

Proponents of mass government surveillance programs say the fact that there have been only a handful of attacks carried out by radical extremists since September 11 is proof that it works. One successful attack took place at the 117th Boston Marathon, which was held on April 15, 2013. The race, which is the oldest continually contested of its kind, attracted more than twenty-three thousand participants, including many of the world's top distance runners, and thousands of spectators. At approximately 2:49 p.m., two pressure cookers that had been fashioned into improvised explosive devices (**IEDs**) exploded within seconds of each other near the finish line. The blasts destroyed the facades of nearby buildings, killed 3 spectators, and wounded more than 260 others.

Law enforcement agencies instantly coordinated to investigate the attack. Within two days, surveillance analysts who had been poring over photographs and recordings captured by security cameras identified two suspects. The footage showed two men who had entered the area carrying heavy black bags, placed them on the ground near the locations of the explosions, and then left before the blasts without the bags. Stills of the suspects were distributed to authorities and news agencies. The suspects were later identified as Tamerlan

Tsarnaev, a former amateur boxer and family man, and his brother, Dzhokhar, who was enrolled at the University of Massachusetts Dartmouth. The two came from a traditional Muslim family that had originated in Kyrgyzstan, which they had fled to seek asylum in the United States. According to relatives, the Tsarnaev brothers' father apparently avoided religious extremism common among terrorists.

On the night of April 18, investigators received reports that an MIT campus police officer was shot and killed and that a Mercedes SUV was carjacked at gunpoint shortly afterward. They connected these reports to the fugitives. A little after midnight, police received a call from the owner of the SUV, who said that he had been taken hostage and forced to withdraw cash from an ATM before escaping when the brothers stopped to fill up at a gas station. The hostage alleged that the brothers were en route to New York City. It has been speculated that the attackers, who were traveling with more IEDs similar to those used in the April 15 bombing, may have been planning to attack New York. The hostage told authorities that they could track the location of his car using the GPS in his cell phone, which he had left in the car.

The police caught up with the Tsarnaevs in Watertown, located just outside Boston, where they exchanged gunfire. The brothers shot at police and threw explosives at them, seriously wounding one officer. Tamerlan Tsarnaev was mortally wounded in the shootout in Watertown, and police eventually cornered Dzhokhar, who had fled after the shootout and hid in a boat that was being stored in a backyard. Dzhokhar was arrested and later stood trial in Massachusetts, where a jury sentenced him to death in the spring of 2015.

Case Study: Slipping Through the Cracks

Although law enforcement officials did not stop the Boston bombing from happening, surveillance played a key role in the investigation and prosecution of the attack. Although police had gathered eyewitness testimony, surveillance footage gave authorities a more complete picture of the event. Specially trained analysts combing through this footage pinpointed two suspicious individuals in a crowd of thousands. In addition, the ability to track a person's cell phone (albeit with their permission) proved invaluable in helping police narrow down and ultimately corner the Tsarnaevs before they could escape into hiding or continue on to attack another location.

The question remains, if there is such a robust network of mass surveillance, how could this attack have happened in the first place? For one thing, no program—let alone a government program—has 100 percent perfect results. Even well-funded and broad programs are bound to have cases like the Boston bombing that slip through the cracks. The nature of *this* case, in particular, lent itself to being overlooked by authorities. The Boston bombing was unique among terrorist attacks because its perpetrators did not fit the common mold of terrorist agents. The Tsarnaevs, though Muslim, were not fundamentalists and did not seem to advocate an extremist attitude about their religion before the attack. Dzhokhar was a naturalized American citizen and was considered to be a fairly successful and well-liked college student. Neither Tamerlan nor Dzhokhar identified with any of the number of Islamic extremist groups operating around the world but

Mass surveillance programs helped police identify and track down the Boston Marathon bombers.

instead worked together to hatch this plot. All of these reasons suggest that the Tsarnaevs were not conventional terrorists, which may help explain why they did not raise suspicion.

It has not been proven whether government surveillance programs are the reason there have been so few attacks in the United States since 9/11. It is possible that there have been many potential attacks that have been thwarted, which would prove the efficacy of surveillance programs. Or it could be that fewer attacks are being planned, which would suggest that surveillance programs do little to stop attacks from happening. Unfortunately, no government agency publicizes the numbers of attacks that *might* have happened. Only a few instances have been cited where the government has prevented an act of terror thanks to surveillance, An unknown number of cases remain classified. However, one thing is clear: thanks to the surveillance infrastructure in place in Boston, authorities were able to catch the Boston Marathon bombers soon after the attack.

The Need for Mass Government Surveillance

At the beginning of the War on Terror in 2001, it was sufficient for law enforcement officials to focus their attention on the activities of foreigners and those residing in the United States with affiliations to known terrorist organizations. However, over the course of more than a decade, the fight against radical jihadists has changed significantly. More terrorist groups are using the internet more often with greater sophistication, publicizing their ideology to inspire new ranks of members and circulating the know-how to carry out deadly attacks around the world. Most troubling, however, is the deterioration of conventional ideas of membership in these groups and the proliferation of lone wolf attacks. Where once a potential terrorist threat could be identified by, say, a pattern of communication to a known jihadist stronghold or suspicious fund transfers, jihadist-inspired attacks are occurring more often with only the barest hints that the perpetrator was radicalized.

The lines have blurred. Ordinary civilians, including American-born and naturalized citizens living regular lives, now pose the threat of being terrorists. To proponents of mass government surveillance, this is not paranoia; this is reality, and it is unprecedented. In the same way that the threat of the Civil War prompted Abraham Lincoln to suspend the right to habeas corpus, the threats of a global War on Terror in which anyone is potentially victim or perpetrator mean that the United States must reevaluate its position on privacy. America is faced with a choice: protecting privacy or protecting the lives of innocent citizens.

The value of surveillance is undeniable. More robust domestic surveillance programs give law enforcement a greater chance to intercept terrorists before they have the chance to act or, should an attack happen, to capture them before they have the chance to cause more harm, as in the case of the Boston Marathon bombing. However, none of that matters if surveillance's impact on privacy proves more detrimental than its potential to save lives. That does not seem to be the case, however, as the scope of government surveillance programs has had minimal impact on Americans' daily lives.

The Scope of Mass Government Surveillance

When Edward Snowden leaked classified documents revealing that the government had been collecting data

Former NSA contractor Edward Snowden was the source of reports on the breadth of US government surveillance.

about the internet activities of American citizens in bulk, many were surprised at the scope and length of time that the NSA had been gathering intelligence. In January 2014, the *Guardian* newspaper reported that the NSA was intercepting approximately five million missed-call alerts and two hundred million text messages, including contact information, content, and in some cases geolocation data attached to those messages, from around the world every day. It provided evidence that such enormous data mining stretched back years. In fact, the NSA was authorized to begin collecting information about American citizens' communications within days of the September 11 attacks. At the time, NSA operations were limited to phone calls originating in the United States and connecting with numbers registered in Afghanistan, where al-Qaeda was believed to be headquartered. By October 4, the NSA's authorization was taken to include all US phone calls as well as email records of any US citizen, and before the end of that month, the NSA was approaching private telecommunications companies to voluntarily submit **metadata**. It is likely, in other words, that any American who made a phone call, sent a text message, or wrote an email in the years following September 11 had at least part of their

Fast Fact

At the end of 2015, more than one thousand jihadist extremists were being actively investigated by the FBI, according to *Politico* magazine. These cases spanned all fifty states.

communication intercepted, documented, and analyzed by the NSA in some way.

American opinion changed sharply in the aftermath of the NSA leaks. In a 2015 Pew Research Center survey, 93 percent of those polled reported that they believe it is important to be in control of who can get information about them, and 90 percent said they believe it is important to be able to decide what information about them can be collected. In the overwhelming majority of both cases, Americans rated control of both *who* has access to their personal information as well as *what* information those people can access as being "very important." This indicates that Americans widely consider privacy to be among the most valued expectations placed on their government. However, as much as people want their privacy to be respected, the fact that the overwhelming majority of Americans did not realize that their personal emails and phone calls were being documented points to the level of interference mass surveillance has had in everyday life: very little, if any.

When chief agents at the NSA were questioned about the agency's mass domestic surveillance program, they justified it by claiming they did not unduly harass ordinary Americans. Those individuals who were targeted for further investigation, the government argued, were connected to a terrorist plot in some way. In other words, the NSA took the position that if an individual had nothing to hide in their communications and internet activities as they related to national security, they had nothing to fear.

Your Data and Advertisers

The type of information the NSA and other government agencies have been shown to collect is called metadata,

Does Surveillance Work?

In the wake of the leaks of classified NSA documents by Edward Snowden, many Americans were understandably shocked. Responding to public pressure, Congress turned its attention to looking into the activities of the agency, raising the question that was on practically everyone's mind: Do these programs actually make us safer?

Answering that question is difficult. For one thing, a positive response means that the NSA and other agencies have indeed prevented attacks from happening in the first place, but it is practically impossible to prove a future event *would* have happened. On top of that, it is necessary for the agency to show the degree to which its surveillance operations impacted the investigation and prosecution of the possible future event. After all, even a well organized terrorist attack could be thwarted by any number of factors, such as local police conducting an investigation without the use of mass surveillance, members of a community notifying authorities of a neighbor's suspicious behavior, or a terrorist conspirator turning himself in or otherwise backing out of the plan. Even unforeseeable factors that change the way a day unfolds, such as weather, may stop a terrorist attack. Any of these could possibly lead to a foiled plot, all without requiring mass data collection and analysis by the NSA.

Despite the challenges associated with proving the viability of mass surveillance, representatives from the NSA have testified that such programs are indeed essential to their mission. On June 18, 2013, the *New York Times* reported that top national security officers presented two

Director of National Intelligence James Clapper testifies before Congress.

cases of "potential terrorist events" that had been thwarted by surveillance programs. In particular, they mentioned a case in which a group operating out of San Diego, California, sent approximately $8,500 to al-Shabab, a Somali terrorist outfit. One of the coconspirators' phone records, which were collected as part of the bulk data surveillance program, were flagged as suspicious, prompting investigators to look into the group's activities. In the other case, a Kansas City, Missouri, man who had once been convicted of sending money to al-Qaeda was shown to have been contacted by a terrorist leader operating out of Yemen. The two had discussed a plot to blow up the New York Stock Exchange, which was in its early stages of planning by the time authorities intervened.

With these declassified examples as justification, the NSA officials insisted that the surveillance programs were working. During the hearing before the House Intelligence Committee, NSA director General Keith B. Alexander said, "In the twelve years since the attacks on September 11, we have lived in relative safety and security as a nation. That security is a direct result of the intelligence community's quiet efforts to better connect the dots and learn from the mistakes that permitted those attacks to occur on 9/11."

Many people volunteer intimate personal information to websites on a daily basis.

which is generally thought of as "data about data." Metadata is a broad term that includes information from a variety of sources, such as phone calls, text messages, emails, and internet searches. Metadata gleaned from phone records, for example, may include originating and terminating phone numbers, date, time, and duration of phone calls, while email metadata might include "from," "to," and "cc" line addresses. A previously declassified July 10, 2009, report on the President's Surveillance Program, written by the Offices of Inspectors General overseeing the Departments of Defense and Justice, the CIA, the NSA, and the Office of the Director National Intelligence, stated that subject lines and email contents were not authorized to be collected. However, the *Guardian* reported that the Snowden leak demonstrated that email subjects and contents were in fact collected.

Metadata is considered by many to be personal information. After all, a person should be able to give out their phone number or email address only to those from whom they want to receive phone calls or emails, right? That may be how it works in day-to-day life, but the reality is far more complicated.

In addition to the fact that government agencies were collecting personal information of ordinary Americans in the first place, the NSA leak also revealed much about *how* they were doing so. In many cases, the NSA relied on private internet service providers, tech companies, and advertisers to divulge information about their users. In these cases, those Americans whose personal metadata was intercepted by the NSA had actually volunteered their personal information to companies and advertisers.

While a person may give out his or her phone number to an individual or business, that number is always registered with the person's telephone or wireless service providers, just as information about email addresses is registered with email providers. Information about incoming and outgoing calls or sent and received messages—in other words, metadata—is stored by companies like Verizon and Google in order to provide their customers with the services that they expect. Customers volunteer information, such as name, phone number, email address, physical address, credit card information, and more, to these companies when they sign up for such services. In the case of sites such as Facebook and Twitter, individuals often volunteer even more personal information, including personal photos and up-to-the-minute status updates, location, and more.

Complicating the matter of volunteering personal information even more, many tech companies do not make money from service contracts the way a phone company might. Instead, these companies earn the bulk of their money through internet advertising. In the case of the search engine juggernaut Google, about 90 percent of its revenue comes from ads. Google offers companies the opportunity to target specific customers by paying Google to put results related to their business, such as their website or an ad, alongside relevant searches. When a person Googles "vegetarian food," a local vegetarian restaurant that has paid Google might come up as a top hit. However, what's to keep ads from other restaurants that are outside of the user's area from popping up? In many cases, Google collects information about its users from sources such as past searches in order to determine a person's location and preferences. This makes sure that the vegetarian restaurant advertising to the customer is one near the customer.

It's not just tech giants like Google that are compiling user information; practically every website a person visits logs information about them. Websites do this by storing **cookies** in an internet user's browser. Cookies are small files that contain information about a user's visit to a website, including when and for how long they visited, what links within the site they clicked, and personal information a person may have volunteered. Cookies can only be read by the website that has stored them, but the information they log may be kept indefinitely. Ever wonder why an ad for a jacket you had looked at on an internet retailer's website pops up on other websites? Blame cookies.

Metadata analysis and cookies help advertisers build more accurate snapshots of their customers' lives, which helps them craft targeted ads that have a higher chance of getting a user to click on them. However, these methods act like internet tracking devices that threaten an internet user's privacy. According to an article on the marketing website Advertising Age, some web-based advertising groups have guidelines that require their members to offer their customers the option to stop targeted ads. However, in these cases, advertisers may continue to track users.

There is an astounding amount of personal information that Americans willingly (if unknowingly) share with their service providers, tech companies, and advertisers. In this case, that information is being used to advertise products and services to people most likely to use them, padding the pockets of marketers in the meantime. It seems unlikely that this practice is going to change any time soon. On the one hand, it is too lucrative for internet advertisers, who rake in hundreds of billions of dollars every year; on the other hand, Americans are too willing to volunteer their personal information in exchange for the convenience of free internet services. (If all this were to change, and Google could no longer offer targeted ads to its customers, it would likely have to start offering an ad-free search engine that charged every time a person looked something up.)

If all of this information is going to be collected anyway, why shouldn't the NSA also have a look at volunteered information in order to help stop crimes or catastrophic terrorist attacks?

John Adams championed the principle that people should be presumed innocent until proven guilty.

CHAPTER 3

The Cons: Presumption of Guilt

As many reasons as there are in favor of mass government surveillance, there are still a number of people who argue that it causes more harm than it is worth. Those who defend privacy do so for both principled and practical reasons. History has shown that surveillance programs are all too easily abused by those directing them; instead of protecting people, surveillance can be used to advance political agendas and personal vendettas. Current headlines demonstrate that government surveillance programs tend to have unintended consequences, including especially the introduction of security vulnerabilities that put ordinary people's data at risk. Lastly, opponents of surveillance frequently contend that such programs contradict essential liberties, including freedom from government interference in private matters, and that they go against the very core of what it means to be an American.

The Principle of Protecting Innocence

Proponents of mass government surveillance programs argue that the increase in the number of lone wolf attacks, particularly those committed by native-born citizens, means that there is a potential for anyone to commit an act of terror. Because lone wolves do not belong to any one extremist group, receive orders, or otherwise make contact with known terrorist organizations, it is difficult to identify them through more conventional surveillance means, such as monitoring phone calls terminating in foreign countries where there is high extremist activity. Therefore, they argue, it is necessary for the government to collect and analyze as much data on its citizens as possible in order to have a chance at picking out and stopping these radicalized individuals before they have a chance to act.

Opponents of government surveillance, meanwhile, contend that this argument goes directly against one of the longest-held values in the American justice system. This principle is known as the presumption of innocence for the accused. One of the most often quoted thinkers on this principle is the eighteenth-century jurist Sir William Blackstone, one of the preeminent legal scholars in the history of English law. Blackstone once said, "It is better that ten guilty persons escape than that one innocent suffer." Blackstone's formulation, as it is known, upholds the idea that a democratic society must protect its citizens from abuses of government power over and against the prosecution of criminals because doing so demonstrates a level of trust between the government and its citizens.

Although Blackstone is perhaps most famous for advocating for this essential right of the accused, he may have been inspired by a far older source: the Bible. The first book of both the Hebrew and Christian Bibles, called Genesis, relates the story of how God wanted to destroy two cities, Sodom and Gomorrah, because the residents there had become sexually deviant and violent. When the human Abraham, whom God had chosen to sire a race of chosen people, heard of God's plan, he had the following conversation with God:

> While the two men walked on farther toward Sodom, the Lord remained standing before Abraham. Then Abraham drew nearer to [God] and said: "Will you sweep away the innocent with the guilty? Suppose there were fifty innocent people in the city; would you wipe out the place, rather than spare it for the sake of the fifty innocent people within it? Far be it from you to do such a thing, to make the innocent die with the guilty, so that the innocent and the guilty would be treated alike! Should not the judge of all the world act with justice?" The Lord replied, "If I find fifty innocent people in the city of Sodom, I will spare the whole place for their sake." Abraham spoke up again: "… What if there are at least ten there?" "For the sake of those ten," he replied, "I will not destroy it." (Genesis 18: 22–32)

Interestingly, God later annihilates the cities, though not before warning the only righteous family there in time for them to escape the destruction.

Unfortunately for humanity, it is not always so easy to achieve absolute justice, with the guilty and the innocent getting what they deserve with perfect accuracy. This quandary is what sparked the principle of protecting the innocent to the fault of letting the guilty go free. This biblical passage parallels Blackstone's formulation, though Blackstone inverts the numbers—instead of saving ten innocents, Blackstone says that the liberty of one innocent must be valued above justice for ten guilty people.

When the founders of the United States were setting forth the laws and principles of a new country, they naturally looked to the history of their former mother country for guidance. As a result, English common law, which was shaped in large part by figures such as William Blackstone, became the foundation for American jurisprudence. The principle of protecting the individual at the expense of punishing crimes was integrated into the tapestry of American law, and many prominent Americans espoused opinions similar to, and in some cases more stringent than, Blackstone's formulation. Among these men was Benjamin Franklin, who served as editor of the Declaration of Independence before it reached the Continental Congress. Franklin so took the principle of protecting innocence to heart that he applied Blackstone's formulation tenfold: "It is better one hundred guilty Persons should escape than that one innocent Person should suffer."

In addition to Franklin, John Adams, who also played a large role in the drafting of the Declaration of Indpendence and later served as the country's second president, also held protecting innocence higher than prosecuting the guilty. His story presents a fascinating take on this essential American value. Revolutionary sentiment in the American colonies, particularly in Adams's home colony of Massachusetts, was coming to a head in the winter of 1770. On the evening of March 5, a group of young patriots in Boston started harassing a British watchman stationed outside of the customs house there. As Captain Thomas Preston ordered seven other soldiers to reinforce the lone watchman, the crowd swelled into a mob. At some point during the riot, a shot was fired. It is not known if it came from one of the British soldiers, who were under orders not to fire their weapons, or from one of the patriots. After the shot, British soldiers opened fire into the crowd, instantly killing three civilians. Two others who had been wounded in the riot later died as a result of their wounds. By the end of the month, Captain Preston and the eight soldiers under his command, as well as several civilians, were indicted by a grand jury to stand trial for murder. Should they have been found guilty, each would have faced the death penalty.

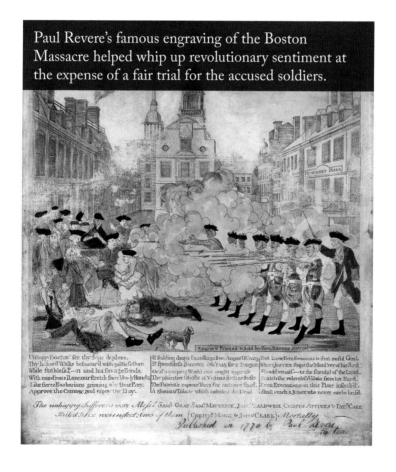

Paul Revere's famous engraving of the Boston Massacre helped whip up revolutionary sentiment at the expense of a fair trial for the accused soldiers.

Tensions in Boston were understandably high, as propagandists like Paul Revere, who dubbed the tragedy "the Boston Massacre," worked to whip up patriot furor in the city. The British soldiers tried and failed to find legal representation in the trial. Ultimately, they found counsel in the most unlikely place: local Boston attorney John Adams, along with his colleague Josiah Quincy, both of whom were revolutionary sympathizers. Although Adams and Quincy did not support the behavior of the British as a whole, they saw that Captain Preston and his men were being denied access to the fairness that many in the colonies were seeking themselves. It would be hypocritical, in other words, for Americans to advocate for liberty while at the same time denying it to others. During the trial, Adams said the following:

> It is more important that innocence be protected than it is that guilt be punished, for guilt and crimes are so frequent in this world that they cannot all be punished. But if innocence itself is brought to the bar and condemned, perhaps to die, then the citizen will say, "whether I do good or whether I do evil is immaterial, for innocence itself is no protection," and if such an idea as that were to take hold in the mind of the citizen that would be the end of security whatsoever.

Adams' argument proved compelling in the end. Captain Preston was found not guilty, with the judge finding that the jury had "reasonable doubt" over his responsibility for the massacre. (The phrase "reasonable doubt," which has since been used as the watermark to determine guilt in criminal proceedings, was first used at the Boston Massacre trials.) Six of the soldiers under Preston's command were also found not guilty of murder, and the remaining two were found guilty of a reduced charge of manslaughter and were therefore spared execution.

The presumption of innocence is both one of the most important foundational principles of American democracy and jurisprudence, and also a highly unusual one. There is a reason why American juries at criminal trials are tasked with finding someone either "guilty" or "not guilty" instead of "innocent" or "not innocent"; the burden of proof falls on the prosecution, which must demonstrate to the jury, in the words of the Boston Massacre trials, *beyond a reasonable doubt* that the accused is guilty. In many other countries, the opposite is true: a person standing trial is presumed guilty, which forces the accused to demonstrate that he or she did not commit the offenses he or she has been accused of. The difference between these two approaches is vast. One takes liberty as its guiding value, while the other, justice.

Fast Fact

The NSA costs American taxpayers between $8 billion and $10 billion a year, according to a 2013 CNN Money article. The NSA's budget, like those of other intelligence agencies, is classified and is not openly debated by Congress, but some, including former White House budget official Gordon Adams, suggest it may cost upwards of $20 billion.

Law enforcement officers must attain a warrant before searching a person's home or belongings.

The presumption of innocence is an imperfect principle. On the one hand, it leads to an abundance of trials in which someone who is actually guilty gets off because of prosecutorial incompetence or a violation in investigative procedure; on the other hand, it does not guarantee that innocent people escape punishment for crimes they did not commit, though it goes a long way toward ensuring that cases of wrongful conviction are minimized. Even though the American justice system is far from perfect, the founders long ago agreed that it was the best available to society.

Mass government surveillance programs, such as the NSA's PRISM program, unravel this core American principle by treating all citizens as a potential threat to the country. Like criminals being investigated for a crime or on parole, their every movement is watched, every moment scrutinized. The principle of presumption of innocence is purposefully designed to make it difficult for the government to investigate and prosecute crimes. The Fourth Amendment, in particular, protects innocence by preventing authorities from carrying out unreasonable searches of private citizens and seizures of private property. Under normal circumstances, law enforcement agents need to acquire warrants, which must be approved by judges. While individual judges may tend to rule in favor either of citizens or the authorities when it comes to approving warrants, the authorities must always provide some sort of compelling evidence that makes it likely that someone has committed, will commit, or is connected to a crime. In the case of mass government surveillance, however, authorities are given access to personal information of all people, regardless of whether they are guilty or innocent. In the same way people do not deserve to be punished for crimes they did not commit, innocent people do not deserve to be treated like suspects in an unending War on Terror when they have done nothing to warrant suspicion. To paraphrase John Adams, surveillance fosters the idea that whether or not a person is a terrorist or a law-abiding citizen does not matter, as they are both treated the same.

Abuse of Power

Imagine being granted access to someone's personal online account, where they store their email and instant messaging apps, their calendar, their internet browser and search history, and their documents. What sorts of things could be learned about this person? The email and messages would reveal who they correspond with and their contact information; the subjects of those messages and their internet history might show what their interests are; their calendar would show where they've been and where they will be going; their documents might show who they are, what they do, and what they're thinking about. All of this information could be collected and used to form a pretty well rounded picture of their identity.

There is enormous power in being able to survey an individual's personal life. By handing that power to the government and allowing law enforcement officers to access personal information, it may help to identify potential threats to national security, but it also runs the risk of having that information used against the individual. History has shown that this level of personal access can result in not only prosecution of real threats but also persecution of innocent individuals. Such persecution is often politically motivated and may have no bearing on the stated reasons for surveillance.

As much as surveillance is a tool for investigating threats to national security, it is all too often abused as a tool for political vendettas and public manipulation.

The secret NSA PRISM program, revealed in Edward Snowden's 2013 leak, is hardly the first instance of mass government surveillance in the United States. The political value of domestic spying has had a long history stretching back decades. The 1950s and 1960s were politically fraught decades defined by the building tension between the democratic United States and the communist Soviet Union in the wake of World War II, as well as by the growing civil rights movement that demanded equality for black Americans. Many at the highest levels of government, including especially presidents John F. Kennedy, Lyndon Johnson, and Richard Nixon, feared that communist spies had infiltrated everyday life and were working diligently to destroy the government from within—not unlike the modern fear of lone wolf terrorists popping up in the United States. As a matter of national security, Congress formed the House Un-American Activities Committee (HUAC) to investigate individuals suspected of espousing communist ideology, including a number of leftist college professors, Hollywood actors and directors, writers, and other artists. Among the chief proponents of this crusade was Senator Joseph McCarthy, whose anticommunist campaign was so severe that it was later dubbed a "witch hunt." (In 1953, American playwright Arthur Miller, himself "blacklisted" for refusing to testify before a HUAC hearing, wrote *The Crucible*, which equated McCarthyism with the witch mania in Salem, Massachusetts, of the late seventeenth century, in which twenty innocent people were executed on charges of occult affiliation.)

Martin Luther King Jr. became the subject of an FBI investigation because of his work for civil rights.

In the 1960s, J. Edgar Hoover, the first director of the FBI, used domestic surveillance as a means to assassinate the character and standing of his political enemies. The most famous of these was Dr. Martin Luther King Jr. Hoover received authorization to investigate King from Kennedy's White House under the Racial Matters Program, which was instituted to oversee individuals like King who were involved in the civil rights movement. In 1962, Hoover raised suspicion that one of King's closest advisers, a man named Stanley Levinson, was "a secret member of the Communist Party." Attorney General Robert Kennedy, JFK's brother, permitted Hoover to install wiretaps in King's home and at the Southern Christian Leadership Conference offices where King worked.

Over time, Hoover seemed to develop a personal vendetta against King that went beyond his professional responsibility to protect the nation, calling King the "most notorious liar in the country." After King delivered his famous "I Have a Dream" speech in 1963 and he became the most prominent leader of the civil rights movement, the FBI's clandestine mission against him began to morph. What started as an investigation into the political leanings of King and his associates turned into a targeted effort to discredit him and thereby erase the moral superiority of the civil rights movement, which had started to disrupt national politics.

The primary tool the FBI used in its campaign to ruin King's character was surveillance. After King's rise to stardom, Hoover considered King to be "the most dangerous negro" living in the United States, historian David Garrow wrote in an email to the *Washington Post*. According to the American Civil Liberties Union report titled "History Repeated: The

Dangers of Domestic Spying by Federal Law Enforcement," "The FBI harassed and investigated Dr. Martin Luther King, Jr. for decades in order to destroy his reputation. The FBI saw him as a potential threat because he might 'abandon his supposed "obedience" to white liberal doctrines (non-violence)."'As a result, Hoover authorized those field offices under his command to expand the surveillance infrastructure around King, installing wiretaps in hotels and offices he visited in addition to those already placed in his private home and office. All of this was done without the knowledge of Attorney General Kennedy, who had originally given the OK to investigate King's ties to the Communist Party. During the course of the investigation, the FBI discovered that King had had several extramarital dalliances and threatened to publicize them if he did not end his involvement in the civil rights movement. The federal government, in other words, was using information gained from surveillance in order to blackmail a private, law-abiding citizen.

In 1976, the United States Senate formed the Select Committee to Study Governmental Operations with Respect to Intelligence Activities (also known as the "Church Committee"). The committee found that Hoover's "extensive surveillance program" against King continued until his assassination in 1968, "employing nearly every intelligence gathering technique at the Bureau's disposal." "No holds were barred," William Sullivan, head of the FBI's domestic intelligence division during the King surveillance program, testified. "We have used [similar] techniques against Soviet agents. [The same methods were] brought home against any organization against which we were targeted. We did not differentiate. This is a rough, tough business."

The treatment of Martin Luther King Jr. by the federal government during the 1960s today serves as a cautionary tale for mass government surveillance programs. The FBI's investigation shows how quickly and easily government power can spiral out of control. What began as an investigation justified by a perceived threat to national security eventually devolved into a situation in which an individual, J. Edgar Hoover, used his authority to prosecute a personal feud with racially discriminatory undertones.

Initially, Attorney General Kennedy, acting on behalf of the president, gave Hoover permission to use the government to look into the political leanings of a private individual. Hoover took Kennedy's inch and stretched it into a mile, however, abusing his significant power to unilaterally expand the investigation into King without Kennedy's knowledge or permission. Hoover's abuse points to the fact that, even though the government often seems like a monolithic entity that works without bias, it is nevertheless comprised of individuals who are as flawed and shortsighted as any of us. The difference is that these individuals are given enormous power, which gives them the ability to not only execute the monumental task of running a country but also to exercise their whims. The Founding Fathers initially struggled to define the right balance of government power with individual liberty because they understood how easy it was for a well-meaning state to abuse the power given to it by its people. As the saying goes, the road to hell is paved with good intentions.

Today, the federal government is again interfering in the activities of another popular civil rights movement, Black Lives Matter. According to the group's website, Black Lives Matter began in response to the 2013 acquittal of George

Zimmerman, who had been charged with the murder of an unarmed black teenager named Trayvon Martin. Black Lives Matter has since grown into a national movement designed to bring attention to the plight of black individuals and communities, including the disproportionate incarceration of blacks and killings of blacks by police and vigilantes. In the lead-up to a planned Black Lives Matter demonstration at the 2016 Republican National Convention, reports based off of Freedom of Information Act requests indicated that the FBI and the Department of Homeland Security had been using their considerable domestic surveillance resources to, among other things, track the social media feeds and physical location of the movement's members. Just as with Hoover's investigation of King's associations with communism, there has been little to suggest that Black Lives Matter harbors or otherwise sympathizes with enemies of the United States, which is the most often cited justification for such programs. There is worry among protestors that such targeted oversight threatens members' First Amendment rights to free speech and assembly, widely considered to be the most prized rights due to American citizens. Activity meant to monitor Black Lives Matter may in fact create an environment in which the movement is snuffed out or else provokes enough outrage that peaceful protests deteriorate into open hostility.

Proponents of mass government surveillance may argue that in a society where all are watched, all are watched equally. The blackmailing of Dr. Martin Luther King Jr. during the civil rights movement, the blacklisting of antiwar protestors during the Cold War and Vietnam, and the violation of the Democratic Party's privacy during Nixon's reelection prove that even in the United States, surveillance is a tool used as

Reports have shown that law enforcement officials are targeting members of the Black Lives Matter movement.

often for political advancement of empowered elites as it is for protecting the nation's security. In the words of David Garrow, "the richly documented history" must be "a well-remembered reminder that US intelligence agencies should not be trusted to behave properly, or even legally, in the absence of aggressive investigative oversight."

Unintended Consequences of Surveillance

The ability of mass domestic surveillance programs to protect the United States against jihadist terror is questionable at best, but there is substantial evidence to indicate that such programs in fact weaken the security of ordinary Americans' data. One of the justifications for robust internet surveillance programs centers around encryption, which, as chapter 2 discusses, protects internet communications such as messages, emails,

> ### Fast Fact
>
> In a 2014 report, the bipartisan Privacy and Civil Liberties Oversight Board, operating within President Obama's administration, could not identify "a single instance involving a threat to the United States in which the [telephone records] program made a concrete difference in the outcome of a counterterrorism investigation." The report continued to say that there has been "no instance in which the program directly contributed to the discovery of a previously unknown terrorist plot or the disruption of a terrorist attack."

banking information, transactions between users and websites, and much more. Those who worry about terrorists' ability to plan and execute attacks on US soil believe that encryption stands in the way of agencies like the NSA, and that if such agencies could only crack these codes, more terrorists could be intercepted and attacks foiled.

The problem is that radical jihadists make up the barest sliver of people who benefit from encryption; everyone who uses the internet, no matter how advanced or casual their use may be, benefits from encryption. Take online shopping, for example. When you order something from a company's web store, you are transmitting information to that company, including your name, what you want, where you want it shipped, how you are paying for it, and where to send the bill. Such information can be very compromising if it falls into the wrong hands. In order to protect it while it's communicated to the retailer, the information is encrypted, which scrambles the data in a way that (hopefully) only the business can read. This process happens regardless of whether the customer is a criminal or an innocent civilian, and it helps to ensure that the internet is a trustworthy place to conduct business.

Government agencies, especially the NSA, have recognized the value of being able to get around encrypted communications ever since the internet first went mainstream in the 1990s. During that decade, the NSA, acting under President Bill Clinton's administration, suggested installing "**clipper chips**" in every phone and computer manufactured in the United States. These chips were purpose-built to give the NSA a "back door" into the encryption processes happening within every device, effectively allowing the government to collect all information stored in and transmitted by any phone

Case Study: Apple, Inc. vs. the FBI

Following the December 2, 2015, attack in San Bernardino, California, the FBI recovered an iPhone 5C belonging to Syed Farook, one of the shooters. The FBI asked Apple, the phone's manufacturer, to provide a back door in order to get around a security feature of the password-protected device that automatically wipes clean the information stored on it after ten unsuccessful attempts to unlock it. The FBI believed that Farook's phone might provide valuable information relating to national security, such as contacts or information relating to further attacks.

Despite the FBI's justifications, Apple refused. The tech company argued that the FBI forcing its software engineers to write this code violated the First Amendment rights to free speech. (Litigation around the clipper chip proposals of the 1990s established the precedent that code qualifies as speech.) Apple also said that introducing a back door to its software would amount to programming a security vulnerability that would potentially put all of its customers' devices at risk, with CEO Tim Cook calling it "a master key, capable of opening hundreds of millions of locks." Whether or not the FBI would abuse the ability to unlock iPhones was beside the point. Apple iPhones are sold all over the world, including in China, where mass government surveillance is more commonplace and where the government has been pushing Apple for greater control of its encryption technology. By granting the FBI a back door, Apple would essentially have to do the same in China, thereby damaging the company's rapport with its customers there.

The standoff eventually led the Justice Department, which represented the FBI, to take Apple to court. Dozens of other Silicon Valley companies, including Google, Facebook, and Microsoft, submitted briefs stating their support for Apple. However, though a hearing was scheduled for March 22, 2016, the Justice Department requested that it be postponed, saying that it may no longer need Apple to give the FBI access. It was later confirmed that the FBI had managed to find another way into Farook's iPhone, potentially through a preexisting vulnerability. The FBI has yet to explain how it circumvented Apple's password protection, leaving many to worry that all Apple devices could potentially be compromised.

Apple's refusal to program a backdoor into the iPhone found widespread support among tech companies and consumers.

or computer. The NSA proposed installing these clipper chips *publicly*, arguing that the growing influence of the internet meant that traditional surveillance technologies that had been used for years, such as wiretaps on landline phones, would soon be obsolete, thereby putting the United States' national security apparatus at a disadvantage.

The clipper chip idea was never officially dropped, with the Clinton administration offering revised proposals as time wore on. None of these were adopted thanks to a diverse coalition of technology manufacturers such as Apple and Netscape, internet "**hacktivists**," and Republican partisans. Senator John Ashcroft, speaking in 1997, some years after the initial "clipper chip" debate, explained the diverse interests involved in squashing the proposal:

> This proposed policy raises obvious concerns about Americans' privacy, in addition to tampering with the competitive advantage that our US software companies currently enjoy in the field of encryption technology. Not only would Big Brother be looming over the shoulders of international cyber-surfers, but the administration threatens to render our state-of-the-art computer software engineers obsolete and unemployed.

Although the NSA failed to win public support for installing what were essentially spy chips in every American-made device, that didn't stop the agency from exploring decryption in other ways. The lesson the NSA took from the clipper chip proposals of the 1990s, it seems, was not that the American people don't want the government to observe

John Ashcroft served as attorney general under George W. Bush during the passage of the USA PATRIOT Act.

every transaction on their connected devices, but that they simply didn't want to *know* about it. According to the leaks provided by Edward Snowden, government agencies such as the NSA have since invested a lot of time, energy, and money into circumventing these common protections in order to gain access to information protected by encryption. They do so unilaterally, without bothering to publicize their activities. Today, the NSA has accomplished this task. According to *ProPublica*:

> The agency has circumvented or cracked much of the encryption, or digital scrambling, that guards global commerce and banking systems, protects sensitive data like trade secrets and medical records, and automatically secures the e-mails, Web searches, Internet chats and phone calls of Americans and others around the world.

This revelation raises concerns in the minds of many who dislike the idea of government oversight in their private matters, but proponents of mass government surveillance argue that such decryption policies mean little to ordinary people. The majority of internet communications, they say, do not have any relevance to national security—in other words, if you have nothing to hide, then you have nothing to worry about.

Even if government agencies use only information relevant to the investigation of terrorists, the fact that the NSA has hacked the encryption that protects day-to-day information has serious repercussions for the average citizen. All code has vulnerabilities in it, which is why software manufacturers such as Apple and Google recommend that their users regularly update their operating systems in order to close holes that they have discovered in their software's security. The NSA has kept knowledge of the security vulnerabilities of encryption secret because it is in their interest to keep these holes open so that they may intercept and read the encrypted information. However, this also means that these vulnerabilities remain open to everyone, including rival governments, jihadists, common cyber criminals, and other hostile groups. Take the "back door" metaphor as an analogy. Imagine if the police discovered that the back door to a citizen's house was unlocked or open. They don't bother to notify the homeowner of the open door because the police think this security vulnerability may come in handy should the homeowner get into trouble and the police need to enter the house quickly. However, because the door is unlocked, anyone may gain access to the house as easily as the police can, including burglars or other criminals. Because encryption is now vulnerable, potentially anyone could gain access to sensitive personal information. Name and address, email and text messages, credit card information—all of this is potentially up for grabs by anyone.

The government has justified its hacking of encryption by arguing that it helps to maintain the security of the nation. However, by leaving these vulnerabilities open, the government is actually putting the security of ordinary Americans' personal information at great risk.

Governments and tech companies are expanding to accommodate more and more data.

CHAPTER 4

Ever Faster Computers

The debate between surveillance and privacy in the United States is not a new one. Privacy has been an integral part of American society practically from the beginning. Many of the first European residents in the New World were refugees hoping to escape the political and religious persecution of the overbearing governments of their home countries. Although the United States was eventually founded on the principles of liberty and individual privacy, there has always been the practical responsibility of a government to protect its citizens and its own interests, and that often means curtailing freedoms to maintain security.

This longstanding dilemma has taken on a new, more complicated aspect in the twenty-first century, one that America's founders could not possibly have imagined. Everyday life in the United States is now fundamentally different than it was hundreds of years ago. Digital technology makes conducting business and communicating with people around the world easier and more convenient than ever before, but there is a dark side as well. The technology that makes it easier to coordinate a group of friends to see a movie also allows criminals and terrorists wishing to harm civilians to plan and execute their attacks.

New Surveillance Technologies

The twenty-first century battlefield seems to be taking place more and more in cyberspace, and the government has had to adapt to the tactics and behavior of online jihadists. Unfortunately, this new enemy means that potentially anyone could be convinced to join a jihad by an online recruiter and commit an act of terror. Because anyone could be a terrorist, everyone is now a suspect. In order to respond to the increased public pressure to stop attacks before they happen, the government now investigates everyone, foreign- and American-born alike, collecting their information and analyzing their communications.

These issues—global terrorism, the surveillance state, and individual freedom—do not seem to be going away soon. Since President Bush declared the War on Terror in 2001, global terrorism and the surveillance state have escalated. Al-Qaeda has fragmented, producing the Islamic State, which has embarked on this century's most systematic, organized, and widespread campaign of conquest in the Middle East and terror around the world. Americans have moved more and more of their personal lives into digital space, putting their information more and more at risk of interception by jihadist groups and government agencies alike. The United States has adapted to the changing landscape, facilitating a sort of cyber arms race that seems to demonstrate its intention of doubling down on domestic surveillance programs.

In 2011, President Obama signed a four-year extension to the USA PATRIOT Act, including provisions authorizing domestic surveillance operations, such as roving wiretaps. Congress briefly allowed these provisions to expire in June 2015, but the following day it passed the USA FREEDOM Act. (Like the USA PATRIOT Act, the USA FREEDOM Act has its own ungainly acronym: Uniting and Strengthening America by Fulfilling Rights and Ensuring Effective Discipline Over Monitoring.) Although the FREEDOM Act restricts the government's ability to collect metadata of private citizens, many of the surveillance programs implemented under the USA PATRIOT Act have new authorization under the FREEDOM Act.

Republican John Thune meets with reporters after a Senate vote to reauthorize the USA PATRIOT Act.

In addition to strengthening its commitment to surveillance through legislation, the United States government has also been funding physical improvements designed to increase its ability to intercept and analyze data. In 2011, the NSA began construction of a multi-billion-dollar data center in Utah (inconspicuously named the Utah Data Center). Although the true cost of the construction of the facility is classified, news reports have suggested that it ranged between $1.5 and $2 billion. Announcement of the building's construction led *Wired* magazine to call the NSA "the largest, most covert, and potentially most intrusive intelligence agency ever." For good reason: the building is the largest of its kind in the world and is designed to house servers capable of storing untold troves of data. Although the Utah Data Center's capacity, like its construction, is classified as a matter of national security, a press release issued by Utah governor Gary R. Herbert has said that it is the "first facility in the world expected to gather and house a yottabyte." (A yottabyte is equivalent to one quadrillion gigabytes. Most personal computers house about five hundred gigabytes of data, which, if Herbet's claim is true, means that the Utah Data Center's capacity is roughly equal to two trillion computers.)

In addition to its enormous data storage capacity, the Utah Data Center also boasts untold computational power. According to mathematician and former NSA employee William Binney in an interview with the *Guardian* newspaper, the Utah Data Center may be able to write, or store, data at a rate of twenty terabytes per minute. That means its computers are fast enough to index the entirety of the Library of Congress in just sixty seconds.

All of this begs the question: For what exactly does the government need all this storage and computational capacity? As with all things involved with national security, the scope and purpose of the Utah Data Center is classified, but the NSA has assured the public that the Utah Data Center will not be used to participate in illegal spying on American civilians. Those outside the spy agency, however, speculate that the facility will be used to store ordinary Americans' information—calls, emails, photos, videos, and more—in large part because the scope of "legal" domestic surveillance in the United States has been greatly expanded in recent years.

Bluffdale, Utah, is home to the NSA's Utah Data Center, the largest data collection facility in the world.

In addition to documenting and storing information, many, including Binney, believe that the NSA may also use the Utah Data Center's cavernous storage capability to proactively hack and decrypt information stored by foreign governments, businesses, individuals, and other targets of interest to the United States government. The prospect of succeeding with such so-called "brute force attacks," however, remains hit or miss. Hard drives, email, and web browsers make use of a robust encryption algorithm known as Advanced Encryption Standard (AES), which utilizes 256-bit technology. The process of decoding encrypted information using a modern computer is based on a trial-and-error approach, which cycles through a randomized set of all possible solutions to a code, trying each one to see if it works. AES is considered so strong that it would take longer than the age of the universe for a modern computer to cycle through all possible solutions to the code.

When it comes to cracking encryption, speed is key—the faster a computer can cycle through all possible solutions to encryption, the sooner that computer will gain access to the information that the encryption is protecting. Recently, the NSA has developed a machine capable of performing a petaflop, or a quadrillion (one thousand trillion) operations calculations each second. At the Multiprogram Research Facility in Oak Ridge, Tennessee, the NSA is hard at work developing a machine capable of exaflop speeds (one quintillion calculations per second). Additionally, computer scientists are working on an experimental new machine known as a **quantum computer**, which, unlike regular computers that encode information as binary bits—1s and 0s—uses qubits (short for "quantum bits"), which are capable of being 1s, 0s,

Activists gather outside the Capitol in Washington, DC, to protest the government's mass domestic surveillance programs in October 2013.

or both at the same time. This flexibility gives them unfathomable processing power.

American Principles in a Changing World

The people who founded America and drafted the country's guiding documents—the Declaration of Independence, the Constitution, and the Bill of Rights—did not set forth a road map for the future. Looking forward from the eighteenth century, they understood that they could not possibly predict what challenges would arise over the next three centuries, let alone what might be around the next decade. Recognizing their limitations, they instead left a framework for government and a set of tools, values, and principles that might help future generations decide how to respond to the unique challenges they would face in their own times. In this way, America is always being refounded by the current generation, adapted and improved to respond to their time's issues.

It is normal to want others in positions of authority to tell us what to think about difficult topics, which is why many people around the world are content to be ruled by a government headed by autocratic leaders. America is not set up in that way. At the end of the day, we cannot know what Thomas Jefferson would have thought about tweets, or what Alexander Hamilton would have thought about bulk telephone metadata collection, or what John Adams would have thought about the clipper chip. And so we cannot look to them to tell us what to do. In a way, America's founders, brilliant though they were, were flawed, and they knew that they were flawed, which is why they left a government that would forever be informed and shaped by *people* living in the world *now*.

America faces unprecedented challenges in the twenty-first century. The War on Terror is unlike any war fought before; the technology that's being developed is unlike anything invented before; the government's surveillance infrastructure is unlike anything used before. This fearful trinity makes up the current situation, and it's up to the current generation of Americans to determine how best to navigate it.

President Obama comments on Russian hacking in the months leading to the 2016 presidential election.

1990s The Clinton administration proposes installing "clipper chips" in all American-made phones and computers. The chips would allow the NSA to intercept digital information before it is encrypted. The proposal ultimately falls by the wayside.

September 11, 2001 Jihadists belonging to the terrorist group al-Qaeda hijack four commercial airliners, flying two into the twin World Trade Center towers in Manhattan, New York, and the third into the Pentagon in Arlington, Virginia, with the fourth having been downed—passengers attempted to regain control of the plane from the hijackers, who then crashed the plane—in an abandoned field before it could reach Washington, DC. Nearly three thousand people die, six thousand are injured, and thousands more would later suffer health complications as a result of the attack, making it the deadliest in American history.

September 20, 2001 President George W. Bush declares a global War on Terror, which would later lead America to fight in Afghanistan and Iraq.

October 26, 2001 President Bush signs the Uniting and Strengthening America by Providing Appropriate Tools Required to Intercept and Obstruct Terrorism (USA PATRIOT) Act into law.

May 2006 *USA TODAY* reports that the NSA, with the help of American telecommunication companies, has been collecting phone call records of tens of millions of Americans.

September 2007 Microsoft becomes the first tech company to cooperate with the NSA's PRISM program, assisting the agency with collecting data on the company's users' search histories, emails, messages, and more.

July 10, 2008 President Bush signs the Foreign Intelligence Surveillance Act (**FISA**) Amendments Act into law. The law retroactively legalizes the NSA's warrantless wiretapping program and provides a legal framework for compelling private technology firms to grant government officials access to communications if one party is suspected of being outside the US.

January 2009 Google begins giving user information to the NSA under the PRISM program.

June 2009 Facebook begins giving user information to the NSA under the PRISM program.

May 26, 2011 President Obama reauthorizes the USA PATRIOT Act, including key elements that authorize domestic spying.

April–May 2012 Leaks reveal that the Department of Justice secretly gathered two months' worth of phone records from Associated Press offices and reporters.

April 15, 2013 Two brothers detonate improvised explosive devices at the finish line of the Boston Marathon, killing three and wounding hundreds more. Though the perpetrators had been radicalized and espoused jihadist ideology, they bore no allegiance to any terrorist group in particular, making them so-called "lone wolf" terrorists.

June–July 2013 Former CIA analyst and NSA contractor Edward Snowden releases evidence detailing the scope of the United States government's massive domestic surveillance programs.

May 2014 The NSA completes construction of the Utah Data Center, a facility designed to collect and analyze the largest amount of data acquired through surveillance in the world.

December 2, 2015 A married couple shoots and kills fourteen people at a Department of Public Health Christmas party held at the Inland Regional Center in San Bernardino, California, before being gunned down by police.

December 2015–March 2016 Apple refuses to grant FBI investigators a "back door" to access the iPhone that had belonged to one of the San Bernardino shooters, saying that the order violated their First Amendment rights and could potentially open all phones to government attack. The FBI eventually withdraws its complaint before going to court, saying it had gained access through an existing vulnerability, but the FBI refuses to tell Apple what it was.

al-Qaeda A radical jihadist militant organization founded in the 1980s. Al-Qaeda initially started in opposition to Soviet intervention in Afghanistan, but after the fall of the Soviet Union, al-Qaeda continued to resist foreign intervention, especially American, in Islamic lands, eventually declaring holy war on the United States and its allies.

amendment A change or addition to a legal document, such as the US Constitution.

asylum Protection granted by a nation to an individual who has fled his or her home nation.

Bill of Rights The first ten amendments to the US Constitution.

bug A small listening device usually consisting of a microphone that is concealed in a telephone or room and used for surveillance.

clipper chip A microchip designed by the NSA as an encryption device that would allow authorities to tap a phone or computer and read its information before it could be encrypted.

constitution A set of laws and beliefs by which a nation or state is governed. The document that organizes the United States government and establishes its principles was adopted in 1789.

cookies A packet of data sent to a browser by an internet server that is used to identify and track a user.

data Information in numerical form that can be sent or processed digitally.

encrypted Information or data that has undergone a proccess of encoding to prevent unauthorized access.

extradite To hand over a person accused of a crime to the state in which the crime was committed.

FISA Foreign Intelligence Surveillance Act; a bill passed by the US Congress in 1978 and amended in 2008 that outlined the procedures for the surveillance of "foreign powers" and their "agents"; FISA has since been used to justify monitoring communication between American citizens and those residing outside the United States.

hacktivists Computer hackers who use their skills to gain access to information and advance a cause.

hijack To illegally seize a vehicle, such as an aircraft, while in transit and to alter its heading for one's purpose.

IED Improvised explosive device; a simple bomb made from common items, especially one used by someone without authority.

ISIS Islamic State of Iraq and Syria; a militant jihadist group, spun off from al-Qaeda, whose goal is to implement a fundamentalist Islamic caliphate in the Middle East.

jihad Arabic word meaning "holy war" or fight against the enemies of Islam; jihad has been used by extremist organizations to justify acts of terror. A jihadist is someone who takes part in a jihad.

lone wolf A person who has been inspired by jihadist propaganda to commit acts of terror but who does not belong to any terrorist organization in particular.

metadata "Information about information"; generally includes originating and terminating phone numbers, date, time, and duration of phone calls, as well as addresses associated with emails.

NSA National Security Agency; a government agency founded after World War II to gather intelligence and decode encrypted transmissions from around the world.

quantum computing An experimental computation system that uses qubits, which render data in terms of 1s, 0s, or both at the same time (as opposed to bits, which render data in terms of 1s and 0s), allowing quantum computers to process more data more quickly than conventional computers.

radicalized Someone who has adopted radical positions on political issues through the influence of others.

surveillance Observation, especially of someone suspected of committing or planning to commit a crime.

terrorism The illegal use of violence or intimidation in order to advance political ends.

USA PATRIOT Act A bill passed by Congress after the terrorist attacks on September 11, 2001, that granted government agencies broad powers to intercept communications around the world in order to prosecute the War on Terror; stands for the Uniting and

Strengthening America by Providing Appropriate Tools Required to Intercept and Obstruct Terrorism Act.

whistleblower A person within an organization who presents evidence or otherwise informs on illegal or suspect activities of that organization.

wiretap To install a listening device, especially on a phone line, in order to conduct surveillance.

writ of habeas corpus A legal right afforded to prisoners who believe that they have been detained illegally in which they present their custodian with a summons bearing the weight of a court order that allows the prisoner to appear before a court.

Books

Boghosian, Heidi. *Spying on Democracy: Government Surveillance, Corporate Power, and Public Resistance.* San Francisco: City Lights Books, 2013.

Greenwald, Glenn. *No Place to Hide: Edward Snowden, the NSA, and the U.S. Surveillance State.* New York: Metropolitan Books, 2014.

Rosen, Jeffrey, and Benjamin Wittes, eds. *Constitution 3.0: Freedom and Technological Change.* Washington, DC: Brookings Institution Press, 2013.

Solove, Daniel J. *Understanding Privacy.* Cambridge, MA: Harvard University Press, 2010.

Websites

American Civil Liberties Union: Privacy and Surveillance

https://www.aclu.org/issues/national-security/privacy-and-surveillance

The American Civil Liberties Union (ACLU) is a legal organization devoted to protecting the essential rights of Americans, including privacy. This website is a great jumping off point for students researching mass government surveillance programs, and it includes a number of subtopics, including relevant videos, statements by governments and citizen groups alike, and even court cases.

The *Guardian*: Edward Snowden

https://www.theguardian.com/us-news/edward-snowden

When NSA contractor Edward Snowden went public with his leak of classified documents outlining the scale of the US government's domestic spying programs, he did so with the *Guardian* newspaper, operating out of the United Kingdom. Ever since, the *Guardian* has been on the frontlines of the modern debate over security, surveillance, and privacy. Its website boasts some of the most exhaustive reporting on Snowden and the NSA leaks and is a great resource on surveillance topics.

National Security Agency

https://www.nsa.gov

This site explains the operations of the NSA and details its activities from the government's point of view.

Books

Greenwald, Glenn. *No Place to Hide: Edward Snowden, the NSA, and the U.S. Surveillance State*. New York: Metropolitan Books, 2014.

Online Articles

Baker, Aryn. "Why Al-Qaeda Kicked Out Its Deadly Syria Franchise." *Time*, February 3, 2014. http://time.com/3469/why-al-qaeda-kicked-out-its-deadly-syria-franchise.

Ball, James. "NSA Collects Millions of Text Messages Daily in 'Untargeted' Global Sweep," *Guardian*, January 16, 2014. https://www.theguardian.com/world/2014/jan/16/nsa-collects-millions-text-messages-daily-untargeted-global-sweep.

Bamford, Sam. "The NSA Is Building the Country's Biggest Spy Center (Watch What You Say)." *Wired*, March 15, 2012. https://www.wired.com/2012/03/ff_nsadatacenter.

"The Boston Massacre Trial." John Adams Historical Society. Accessed October 13, 2016. http://www.john-adams-heritage.com/boston-massacre-trials.

"Breaking Down Apple's iPhone Fight With the U.S. Government." *New York Times*, March 21, 2016. http://www.nytimes.com/interactive/2016/03/03/technology/apple-iphone-fbi-fight-explained.html.

Burrington, Ingrid. "A Visit to the NSA's Data Center in Utah." *Atlantic*, November 19, 2015. http://www.theatlantic.com/technology/archive/2015/11/a-visit-to-the-nsas-data-center-in-utah/416691.

Capaccio, Tony. "MLK's Speech Attracted FBI's Intense Attention." *Washington Post*, August 27, 2013. https://www.washingtonpost.com/politics/mlks-speech-attracted-fbis-intense-attention/2013/08/27/31c8ebd4-0f60-11e3-8cdd-bcdc09410972_story.html.

Carroll, Rory. "Welcome to Utah, the NSA's Desert Home for Eavesdropping on America." *Guardian*, June 14, 2013. https://www.theguardian.com/world/2013/jun/14/nsa-utah-data-facility.

Dueholm, James A. "Lincoln's Suspension of the Writ of Habeas Corpus: An Historical and Constitutional Analysis." *Journal of the Abraham Lincoln Association* 29, no. 2 (Summer 2008): 47–66. http://quod.lib.umich.edu/j/jala/2629860.0029.205/--lincoln-s-suspension-of-the-writ-of-habeas-corpus?rgn=main;view=fulltext

"Federal Bureau of Investigation." *King Encyclopedia*, Stanford University. Accessed October 14, 2016. http://kingencyclopedia.stanford.edu/encyclopedia/encyclopedia/enc_federal_bureau_of_investigation_fbi.

Greenwald, Glenn. "NSA Collecting Phone Records of Millions of Verizon Customers Daily." *Guardian*, June 6, 2013. https://www.theguardian.com/world/2013/jun/06/nsa-phone-records-verizon-court-order.

Greenwald, Glenn, and Ewen MacAskill, "NSA Prism Program Taps in to User Data of Apple, Google and Others." *Guardian*, June 7, 2013. https://www.theguardian.com/world/2013/jun/06/us-tech-giants-nsa-data.

Harding, Luke. "How Edward Snowden Went from Loyal NSA Contractor to Whistleblower." *Guardian*, February 1, 2014. https://www.theguardian.com/world/2014/feb/01/edward-snowden-intelligence-leak-nsa-contractor-extract.

Herbert, Gary R. "2012 Energy Summit." Utah.gov. Accessed November 28, 2016. http://blog.governor.utah.gov/2012/02/2012-energy-summit.

History.com staff. "Boston Marathon Bombings," History. com. Accessed October 11, 2016. http://www.history. com/topics/boston-marathon-bombings.

Hutchinson, Alex. "Hacking, Cryptography, and the Countdown to Quantum Computing." *New Yorker*, September 26, 2016. http://www.newyorker.com/tech/ elements/hacking-cryptography-and-the-countdown- to-quantum-computing.

"Ex Parte *Merryman* and Debates on Civil Liberties During the Civil War." Federal Judicial Center. Accessed October 7, 2016. http://www.fjc.gov/history/home.nsf/ page/tu_merryman_bio_merryman.html.

Kaplan, Eben. "Terrorists and the Internet." Council on Foreign Relations, January 8, 2009. http://www.cfr.org/ terrorism-and-technology/terrorists-internet/p10005.

Larson, Jeff, Nicole Perlroth, and Scott Shane. "Revealed: The NSA's Secret Campaign to Crack, Undermine Internet Security." *ProPublica*, September 6, 2013. https://www.propublica.org/article/the-nsas-secret- campaign-to-crack-undermine-internet-encryption.

Levs, Josh, and Holly Yan. "Western Allies Reject ISIS Leader's Threats Against Their Civilians," CNN,

September 22, 2014. http://www.cnn.com/2014/09/22/
world/meast/isis-threatens-west.

Ligato, Lorenzo. "An Embarrassing Number of
People Say They Couldn't Live Without Their
Smartphone." *Huffington Post*, July 13, 2015. http://
www.huffingtonpost.com/2015/07/13/smartphone-
dependence-addiction_n_7785782.html.

Lincoln, Abraham. "A Proclamation on the Suspension of
Habeas Corpus, 1862." The Gilder Lehrman Institute of
American History. Accessed October 7, 2016. https://
www.gilderlehrman.org/history-by-era/american-
civil-war/resources/proclamation-suspension-habeas-
corpus-1862.

Madden, Mary, and Lee Rainie. "Americans' Attitudes
About Privacy, Security and Surveillance," Pew Research
Center, May 20, 2015. http://www.pewinternet.
org/2015/05/20/americans-attitudes-about-privacy-
security-and-surveillance.

McBride, Alex. "Landmark Cases: *Griswold v. Connecticut*
(1965)." PBS. Accessed October 5, 2016. http://www.
pbs.org/wnet/supremecourt/rights/landmark_griswold.
html.

McCullough, Brian. "The NSA and the 1990s Debate Over the Clipper Chip." Internet History Podcast, September 1, 2014. http://www.internethistorypodcast.com/2014/09/the-nsa-and-the-1990s-debate-over-the-clipper-chip.

Montgomery, David, Sari Horwitz, and Marc Fisher. "Police, Citizens and Technology Factor into Boston Bombing Probe," *Washington Post*, April 20, 2013. https://www.washingtonpost.com/world/national-security/inside-the-investigation-of-the-boston-marathon-bombing/2013/04/20/19d8c322-a8ff-11e2-b029-8fb7e977ef71_story.html.

Patterson, Brandon Ellington. "Civil Rights Groups Move to Expose Government Spying on Black Lives Matter." *Mother Jones*, July 5, 2016. http://www.motherjones.com/politics/2016/07/black-lives-matter-government-surveillance-civil-rights.

"Profile: Edward Snowden." BBC, December 16, 2013. http://www.bbc.com/news/world-us-canada-22837100.

"Quartering Act (1765)," United States History.com. Accessed October 4, 2016. http://www.u-s-history.com/pages/h641.html.

"The Quartering Act." US Constitution Online, January 8, 2010. http://www.usconstitution.net/quarteringact.html.

"Quotes." John Adams Historical Society. Accessed October 13, 2016. http://www.john-adams-heritage.com/quotes.

"The Right of Privacy." Exploring Constitutional Conflicts, University of Missouri at Kansas City. Accessed October 4, 2016. http://law2.umkc.edu/faculty/projects/ftrials/conlaw/rightofprivacy.html.

Sahad, Jeanne. "What the NSA Costs Taxpayers." CNN Money, June 7, 2013. http://money.cnn.com/2013/06/07/news/economy/nsa-surveillance-cost.

Savage, Charlie. "N.S.A. Chief Says Surveillance Has Stopped Dozens of Plots." *New York Times*, June 18, 2013. http://www.nytimes.com/2013/06/19/us/politics/nsa-chief-says-surveillance-has-stopped-dozens-of-plots.html?_r=0.

Smith, Aaron. "Chapter One: A Portrait of Smartphone Ownership." *U.S. Smartphone Use in 2015*, Pew Research Center, April 1, 2015. http://www.pewinternet.org/2015/04/01/chapter-one-a-portrait-of-smartphone-ownership.

Swartz, Noah. "How Advertisers' Cookies Are Helping the NSA's Data-Collection Efforts." *Advertising Age*, July 20, 2015. http://adage.com/article/guest-columnists/advertisers-nsa-collect-data/299523.

"Transcript of President Bush's Address." CNN, September 21, 2001. http://edition.cnn.com/2001/US/09/20/gen.bush.transcript.

Vicens, AJ, Dave Gilson, and Alex Park. "How We Got from 9/11 to Massive NSA Spying on Americans: A Timeline." *Mother Jones*, September 11, 2013. http://www.motherjones.com/politics/2013/09/nsa-timeline-surveillance.

"Watergate Scandal." Encyclopedia Britannica Online. Accessed October 6, 2016. https://www.britannica.com/event/Watergate-Scandal.

Page numbers in **boldface** are illustrations. Entries in **boldface** are glossary terms.

Andrew Coddington holds degrees in English, creative writing, and classics and has a background in American law. He has written several books for Cavendish Square on a variety of topics, including American history and politics. He has recently published *Thomas Jefferson: Architect of the Declaration of Independence* in the Great American Thinkers series. He lives in Buffalo, New York, with his wife and dog.